What... Football Job Can You Do?

Emma Juhasz

Mighty Shepherd Publishing

Illustrations by Amanda Lillywhite

Copyright & Acknowledgements

Thank you for your help!
Tay Albayrak (Sports Physiotherapist)
Rob Bowyer (Sports Engineer/Designer)
Brinda Christopher (Sports Doctor)
Luke Craig (Coach)
Amy Crook (Brentford FC)
Aaron Dagger (Sports Analyst)
Chelsey Dempsey (Sports Psychologist)
Piers Edwards (Sports Broadcaster)
Nick Gardener (Coach)
Paddy Harverson
Ray Herb (Referee Association)
Jamie Mackie (Ex-Professional Footballer and Broadcaster)
Harri Stephens (Sports Scientist)
Edward Woodward

AND

Amanda Lillywhite for her wonderful illustrations.

Mike at Ex Why Zed for designing and printing the book.

Published in the United Kingdom by:
Emma Juhasz
www.emmajuhasz.com

Content copyright © Emma Juhasz, 2022
Illustrations copyright © Amanda Lillywhite, 2022

All rights reserved. No portion of the book may be reproduced, stored in a retrieval system or transmitted at any time, or by means, electronic, photocopying, recording or otherwise, without written permission of the publisher.

The right of Emma Juhasz to be identified as the author of the work has been asserted by her in accordance with the Copyright, Design and Patents Act 1988.

A CIP record of this book is available at the British Library.

First Printed: October 2022

Contents

	Page
Football Essentials	5
The Beautiful Game	6
Essential Kit	7
Can You Kick It?	8
What Can You Do?	11
Meet the Team	12
Manager & Coach	16 & 17
Scout & Agent	18 & 19
Player Care & Referee	20 & 21
Club Doctor & Physiotherapist	22 & 23
Sports Nutritionist & Psychologist	24 & 25
Sports Scientist & Analyst	26 & 27
Sports Designer & Media	28 & 29
Club & Grounds Staff	30
Football Focus	33
Football Facts	34
Are Those the Rules?	36
Football Around the World	38
Football Technology	41
Future Footballers	45
Football For Everyone	49
Activities	
Snakes and Ladders Warm-Up	10
Draw Your Own Strip	32
Fast as Lightning	40
Game of Two Halves	44
Make a Table Football	48

About the Author

Emma's children are always asking questions about different jobs, so she decided to write careers books to help all primary-school aged children focus on their futures.

Emma uses her experience as a television documentary-maker and writer, to research and write these books. This is her third book, others in the series are: *What Do Vets Do?* and *What Do Construction Workers Do?*

Emma publishes her own books under Mighty Shepherd Publishing.

Did you know? Emma's surname, *Juhasz*, means *Shepherd* in Hungarian.

What's the picture? A Puli; it's a small, black, hairy Hungarian sheep dog. It looks after the Shepherd's sheep.

For more news and information about Emma and her books visit: www.emmajuhasz.com

Football Essentials

The Beautiful Game
▶ all about football!

Football is the world's most popular game.

More than 265 million men and women play football worldwide. This doesn't include those who play for disabled teams, such as blind, deaf or powerchair football; then there are those who just play for fun! It really is a game for everyone.

There are around 3.5 billion fans; people who watch and support the game; that's about half the world! It is most popular in UK, Europe, Asia, Africa and the Americas.

The biggest football competition is the World Cup. It is held every four years and is the most watched sporting event in the world. The World Cup in 2018 was seen by 3.2 billion people.

Essential Kit

Football Essentials

Football: make sure you get the right size

Size	Age
2	4 to 5
3	7 to 9
4	10 to 14
5	15 to adult

Stopwatch: if you're keeping time of your game.

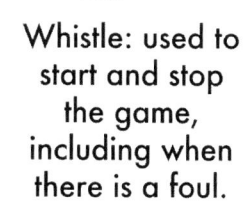

Whistle: used to start and stop the game, including when there is a foul.

Shin Pads: important to prevent injuries from tackles.

Goalkeeper Gloves: help grip the ball and protect your hands.

Football Essentials

Can You Kick It?
▶ *going pro*

Do you want to play football for your job? YES! You need to become a professional footballer, who plays and trains with a club.

Professional Clubs
Across the world, there are around 3,900 clubs in over 200 countries.

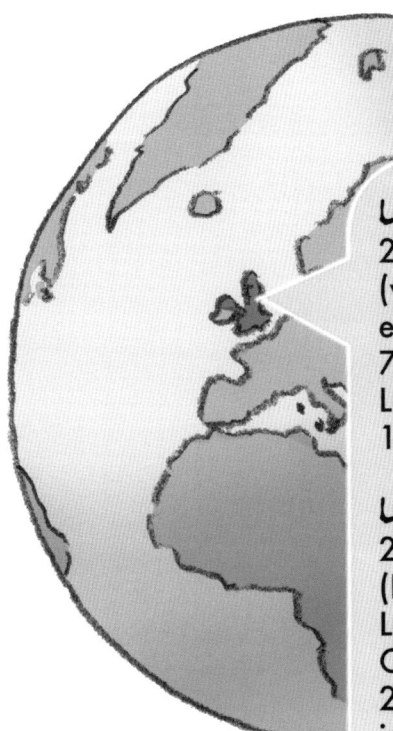

UK men's clubs
20 in the Premier League (with only 25 players in each club squad), 72 in the English Football League, 42 in Scotland, 12 in Wales.

UK women's clubs
24 in England (FA Women's Super League and Women's Championship League), 20 in Scotland and 8 in Wales.

What does it take to become a pro?

* Passion: all you want to do is play football.
* Talent: incredible player.
* Athletic: super fit.
* Attitude: ready to learn, great team player.
* Motivation: always want to play and train.
* Confidence: believe you can do it.
* Sacrifice: football comes first.

Football Essentials

Give it a go to be a pro but just so you know...

less than 1% of children who train in club academies from the age of nine will become a professional footballer.

Don't give up on your dream, but remember that football is a huge industry and there is something for everyone. So read on...!

Snakes & Ladders Warm-up
▶ *activity*

Roll a dice, you can only use numbers 1, 2 and 3, and start your footie warm-up.

You are ready to play!	**11** Hold a ball between your ankles, jump up and down. Repeat 5 times.	**10** Run on the spot as fast as you can, while counting to 20.
7 Do 5 star jumps.	**8** Hop on 1 foot, bounce a ball, and count to 10.	**9** Do 5 push-ups.
6 Do 5 squats.	**5** Throw a ball in the air and catch it 5 times.	**4** Do 5 sit-ups.
Start Here!	**2** Stretch up and then reach down and touch your toes. Repeat 5 times.	**3** Hop on 1 foot while counting to 10.

Football Essentials

What Can You Do?

Meet the Team
▶ jobs in football

What Can You Do?

Iain – Manager
In charge of a club and team.
See page 16 to find out more.

Katie – Coach
Trains a team.
See page 17 to find out more.

Matthew – Scout
Finds new players for a club.
See page 18 to find out more.

Georgie – Agent
Looks after players' careers.
See page 19 to find out more.

Jerome – Player Care
Helps players with their day-to-day needs.
See page 20 to find out more.

What Can You Do?

Amy – Referee
Supervises a football game.
See page 21 to find out more.

Sophie – Club Doctor
Looks after players' health.
See page 22 to find out more.

Taylor – Club Physiotherapist
Prevents and treats injuries.
See page 23 to find out more.

Meet the Team
▶ jobs in football

What Can You Do?

Mona – Nutritionist
Educates players on what to eat.
See page 24 to find out more.

Sacha – Psychologist
Manages players' wellbeing.
See page 25 to find out more.

Rob – Sports Scientist
Creates fitness training plans for players.
See page 26 to find out more.

Aaron – Performance Analyst
Puts together essential information about players.
See page 27 to find out more.

Taha – Sports Designer
Designs footballs and clothes for players.
See page 28 to find out more.

Eva – Sports Media
Writes and talks about football in the media.
See page 29 to find out more.

What Can You Do?

There are many jobs involved in running football clubs and their grounds. Discover some of the main ones.
See pages 30 & 31 to find out more.

Helen – Public Relations

Victor – Groundsman

Manager
▶ *the boss*

What Can You Do?

What do they do?
Managers are in charge of a club's players, money, and reputation (what people think of the club). They decide on training, tactics and the team. They will sign new players, sell (transfer) others to different clubs and work out players' contracts. They promote and discuss the club on television and in newspaper interviews.
Managers are generally experienced ex-players and will also have spent some time coaching.

Coach
▶ team leader

Katie is working out the training plan, for the First Team, with the manager. The manager has decided the team will play in an attacking 4-4-2 formation, which they have put on the tactics board. Now they need to work out what the team needs to practice, so they can beat the opposition.

What Can You Do?

What do they do?
Coaches advise, instruct and encourage players, as well as planning training and organising the team. They can work with any age group from six years old, up to the elite players on the First Team.

Scout

▶ discover new talent

What Can You Do?

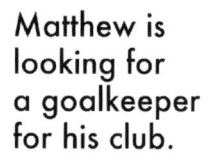

Matthew is looking for a goalkeeper for his club.

He was told about a great one at another club, so he is watching her in a training session. Matthew's club needs a player who can defend as well as goal keep, so Matthew needs to make sure she can kick accurately, tackle well and stop goals being scored.

What do they do?
Scouts find new, exciting, and talented players for their club. They will search for players in local clubs, league teams and in teams around the world.

Agent
▶ manage players' careers

Georgie is with her star player at a primary school near his club; she has arranged for the media to come to watch and photograph him. The player is teaching children some football skills, as he wants to help and encourage younger children to get into football.

What Can You Do?

What do they do?
Agents work for the player. They negotiate contracts with a new club (It includes how long a player will be at the club and how much they'll be paid.). They will organise publicity in the media and sponsorships e.g. the player will be paid to wear a certain sports kit.

Player Care
▶ helping hand

What Can You Do?

Jerome is at the airport meeting a new player who has just flown in from Spain. He will take him to his hotel, then to his medical (tests to make sure he's fit), before taking the player to the club to sign his contract.

What do they do?
Player carers help with everything that's NOT to do with football, so players can focus on training and playing. This can be anything from paying player's bills, planning travel, to finding them a house to live in.

Referee
▶ supervises the match

Amy uses arm signals to communicate with players in a match. Below, Amy is signalling to play an advantage: play does not stop for a foul, as it would affect the non-offending team.

What Can You Do?

What do they do?
Referees make sure a match is played fairly and by the rules. They use a whistle to control the game and will stop it for fouls or penalties. Referees are supported by two assistant referees on the side-lines, a fourth official, and sometimes a VAR (see page 42). They need to be calm and firm when dealing with angry players and managers.

Club Doctor
▶ healthy players

What Can You Do?

Sophie is doing an ultrasound of a player's ankle. He fell during a game, so Sophie needs to see what he has damaged. The ultrasound shows her what is going on inside the player's body. Being able to see exactly what is wrong, helps Sophie work out the best treatment for the player.

What do they do?
Club doctors look after all the players. They constantly check their health, so the players can give their best performance. When one of the team is sick or injured though, they help them recover safely and quickly.

Club Physiotherapist
▶ treating injuries

Taylor keeps a player fit while she is injured by getting her to run on an underwater treadmill. The player has a knee injury and has not played for four weeks. The water supports her weight, so she does not hurt her knee when she runs.

What Can You Do?

What do they do?
Club physiotherapists diagnose and treat players' injuries, then create training plans to help them recover. They get players ready for games with massages and taping any injuries. At matches they will help players if they are hurt.

Club Nutritionist
▶ fuelling players

What Can You Do?

Mona is talking to a chef about the week's menu for the midfielders. A midfielder runs fast and far in training and games, so needs many small meals and snacks during the day.

NO CHOCOLATE OR SWEETS!

PASTA

CHICKEN

What do they do?
Club nutritionists advise every player about what they should eat and drink, as it will affect how they play. They plan what players should eat at the club and at away matches.

Club Psychologist
▶ understanding feelings

Sacha is with a young player who is upset. He asks her to draw a picture and she draws a goal on fire; it shows how angry she is for not scoring in her last five matches. Sacha will talk with her and help her work out how to cope with her feelings.

What Can You Do?

What do they do?
Club psychologists help players of all ages cope with their feelings, such as worry, anger and sadness. Feelings can affect players' games, friendships and home lives, so it's important to talk about them.

Sports Scientist
▶ focus on fitness

What Can You Do?

Rob is training the squad to run faster, so he is making them do a running race. He knows how fast they all ran before, so the squad need to beat each other, as well as their own fastest running times.

What do they do?
Sports Scientists create training plans for players, to make them fitter and faster. Plans are based on GPS vest information (see Page 43), such as heart rate and how far and fast they can run.

Performance Analyst
▶ essential numbers

Aaron is with the coach showing a player footage of his last game. The player is seeing what he did right and wrong, while the coach is looking at the information about the player, which shows her what he needs to practice more in training.

What Can You Do?

Passes on target 55%
Tackles made 34%
Headers won 40%
Crosses 25%

What do they do?
Performance analysts gather information and video footage on players and opposition teams, such as passes on target, headers won, and tackles made. This is used to plan training and tactics to win the next match.

Sports Designer
▶ creating kit

What Can You Do?

Taha is designing a new football boot. Players told him they wanted boots to be light, fast, tough, and accurate when they kick a ball. Taha is testing out his design using a robot foot and leg. The robot kicks the ball from many different angles and shows him how to improve the boot design.

What do they do?
Sports designers create new footballs, shirts, boots, and gloves to help players perform better; they design, test, and redesign an item until it's perfect. New products can take years to develop and make.

Sports Media
▶ football stories

Eva is in a studio presenting a live football match on television; the game has been stopped due to a serious injury and so there is nothing to watch.

Eva is talking into the camera until the game starts again. Many things can go wrong on live television, so a presenter must be calm and prepared for problems.

What Can You Do?

What do they do?
People in sports media can write, present, or create programmes about football. This can be on television, radio, podcasts, websites, social media, newspapers, or magazines. There are many different jobs, such as writer, editor, presenter, cameramen, director, and soundmen.

Club & Grounds Staff
▶ making the club a success

What Can You Do?

Helen, *Public Relations.* Keeps the public updated about the club, such as new kit launches, player transfers and messages from the manager.

Victor, *Groundsman.* Keeps the pitches in perfect condition.

Tracie, *Merchandise.* Promotes and sells the club's clothes and gifts at the stadium, online and abroad.

Alex, *Sponsorship Sales.* Gets companies to support the club, e.g. a company pays to put their logo on the players' kit.

Cheryl, Club Venue Operations Manager. Organises all the staff, before, during and after matches.

Josh, Club Communications. Updates fans with club news on various media.

What Can You Do?

Lin, Membership/Merchandise. Sells tickets for matches and packages for fans to join the club, so they get tickets first, club news and discounts.

Martin, Chef. Cooks at one of the many restaurants at the stadium, which are open before, during and after a match.

Design a Football Kit
▶ activity

What Can You Do?

Colour in the player and his football kit. Use your favourite team's colours, or create a new kit in any colours you like!

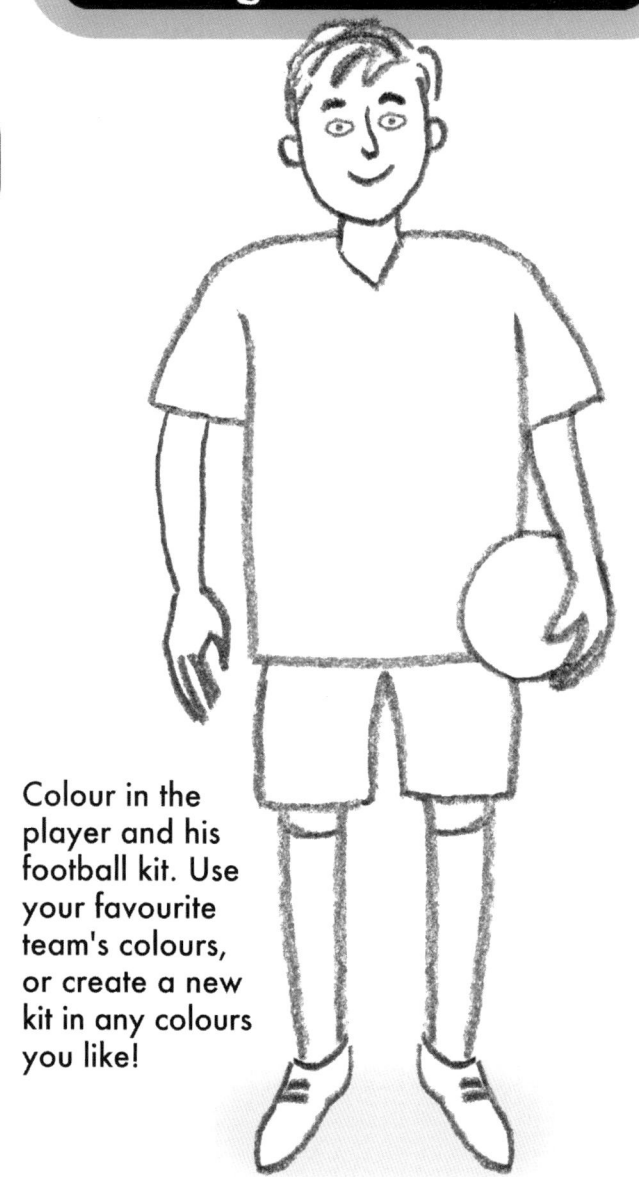

Football Focus

Football Facts
▶ number crunchers

Here are some incredible stats to boot at your friends!

1. 2 mins 56 seconds – fastest hat-trick in a football game. Sadio Mané, Southampton vs Aston Villa in 2015.

2. 11 seconds – fastest World Cup goal. Hakan Sukur, Turkey vs South Korea in 2002.

3. 17 years old – youngest player to participate, score and win a World Cup final. Pelé, played for Brazil in the 1958 World Cup.

4. 36 red cards – most given in ONE game. Claypole vs Victoriano Arenas, Argentinean teams, on 4th March 2011. 22 players, 14 substitutes and coaches were sent off!

5. 476 BC – year football was invented in China. It was first called Cuju.

Football Focus

6. 55 years old – oldest football player. Kazuyoshi Miura (King Kuzu), a former Japan international striker, now plays for Suzuka Point Getters.

7. 96.01 metres – longest goal scored. Goalkeeper Tom King scored from his goal kick, Newport County vs Cheltenham Town, 19th January 2021.

8. 149-0 – highest match score. SO l'Emyrne, a team in Madagascar, purposely lost the game due to an argument with the referee.

9. 165 years – oldest club. Sheffield FC was formed on 24th October 1857.

10. 222 million euros – most expensive transfer. Neymar from Barcelona to Paris Saint-Germain (PSG) in August 2017.

Are those the rules?
▶ what you need to know!

Stay ahead of the game, by knowing some of football's less well-known rules.

✴ Full of Air
If you puncture the ball as you score, the goal does not count. A ball must be fully pumped up for a goal to be allowed.

✴ Red Alert
Referees can send off (red card) players who misbehave while on the pitch, even if the game hasn't started, or if it has already finished.

✴ Every Second Counts
A goalie can only hold onto the ball for a maximum of six seconds.

✶ Smooth Stud

Players will be sent off if their boot studs are not smooth and have sharp edges. This is because they could stab someone with their stud.

✶ Magic Seven

Football teams are usually 11 players, but you can start a game with a minimum of seven, although you may not beat the other team if they have 11!

✶ Five Reds

A 11-a-side team can receive a maximum of four red cards; a fifth red card would stop the game. This is because the team would have less than seven players on the pitch.

✶ Keep Your Shirt On

Players are given a yellow card if they take off their shirt to celebrate after scoring a goal, even if the goal is then not allowed.

Football Around the World
▶ country competitions

These are some of the biggest men's football competitions in the world. Keep watching to see who wins next!

Football Focus

1. The World Cup
Run by FIFA, the governing body that oversees football around the world.
Started: 1930.
Biggest winner: Brazil, 5 times.

2. UEFA European Championships (Euros)
Started: 1960.
Biggest winners: Germany and Spain, 3 times each.

3. Copa America
Started: 1916.
Biggest winners: Uruguay and Argentina, 15 times each.

4. AFC Asian Cup
Started: 1956.
Biggest winner: Japan, 4 times.

5. African Cup of Nations
Started: 1957.
Biggest winner: Egypt, 7 times.

Football Around the World
▶ greatest scorers

These are the world's top scorers, for now. With many more games to come, can you keep count of their goals?

Christine Sinclair
Canada
★ 190 goals ★

Christiano Ronaldo
Portugal
★ 117 goals ★

Football Focus

Women *(from 2nd to 5th highest)*
Abby Wambach: USA, 184 goals
Mia Hamm: USA, 158 goals
Carli Lloyd: USA, 134 goals
Kristine Lilly: USA, 130 goals

Men *(from 2nd to 5th highest)*
Ali Daei: Iran, 109 goals
Mokhtar Dahari: Malaysia, 89 goals
Lionel Messi: Argentina, 88 goals
Ferenc Puskás: Hungary, 84 goals

Fast as Lightning
▶ activity

Try the Bean Bag Dash to get running faster.

Race a friend or get into teams.

Put five bean bags in a line a short distance from each other.

Run, get the first one, run back, tag the next player, or if it's just you, run again!

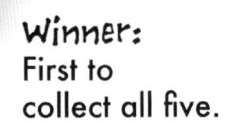

Football Focus

Winner: First to collect all five.

Challenge: Put the bean bags further apart.

Fastest Footballer
Kylian Mbappe ran at 23.61 miles per hour (mph) in a game in 2019, which is faster than Usain Bolt's (world's fastest runner) 100m world record in 2009 – he ran at 23.35mph.

Football Technology

Football Technology
▶ game changers

✶ Goal-line Technology

The referee has a watch linked to 14 cameras all focused on the goal line. When a ball goes over the line, the watch buzzes to tell the referee it's a goal.

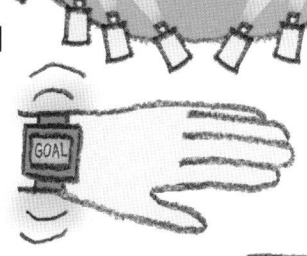

✶ Virtual Assistant Referee (VAR)

Officials who watch a game on screens, look for errors or serious incidents that the referee misses. They will replay the incident on a screen just off the pitch, for the referee to review.

✳ Virtual Reality (VR) Headset

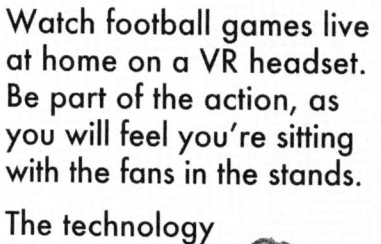

Watch football games live at home on a VR headset. Be part of the action, as you will feel you're sitting with the fans in the stands.

The technology for this has just begun, but it is something to watch out for.

✳ GPS Vest

Worn by players to track and measure everything they do during training and a game. There is an electronic pod between their shoulder blades which connects to an app on an iPhone or iPad. This information is used to help the players get fitter, as well as recover properly from injury.

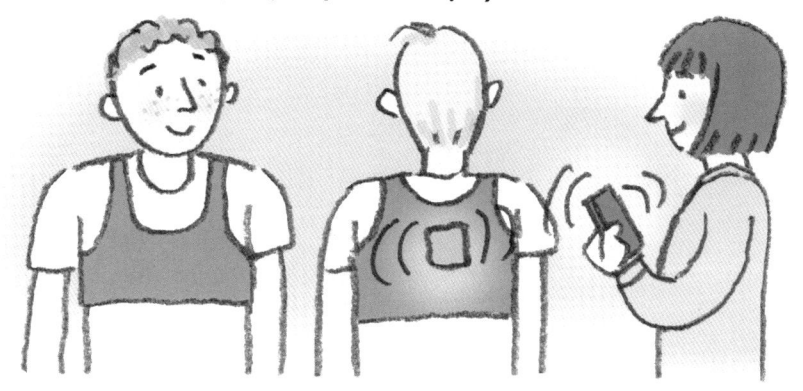

Football Technology

A Game of Two Halves!
> ▶ activity

If you can't always get a team together, here's an idea of how to play with a brother/sister parent or friend. This is not just football though, it's Football Tennis! See below, how to play.

Tie a rope between two chairs to make a 'net'.

Use jumpers to mark out the end of the 'court' on both sides of the 'net'.

Football Tennis (two or more players)

Kick the ball over the 'net', the ball can bounce once, your opponent must kick it back.

Win a point every time your opponent misses, the ball bounces more than once, or it goes out. First to 10 wins.

Future Footballers

Future Footballers
▶ pathway to being a pro

Start here!

For fun
age 5 onwards
Can play for local youth clubs and leagues.

Need to know
You will train, play, and do schoolwork at the club.

At the end of your contract you can be re-signed, or sold to another club, or released to try out for another club.

Play for your country
Elite players can be selected for the U16-20 national youth squad, then the senior national team.

Next level
age 9 onwards

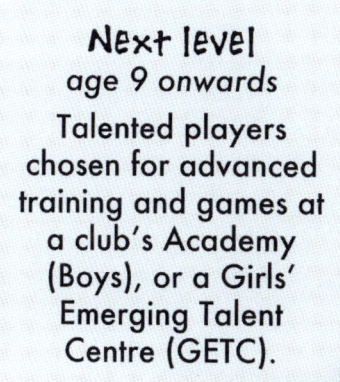

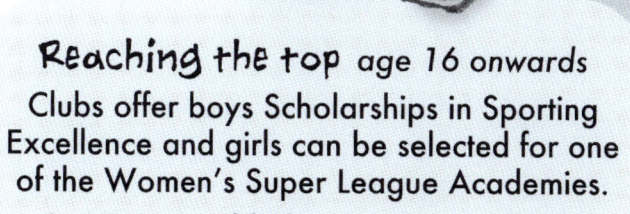

Talented players chosen for advanced training and games at a club's Academy (Boys), or a Girls' Emerging Talent Centre (GETC).

Reaching the top *age 16 onwards*

Clubs offer boys Scholarships in Sporting Excellence and girls can be selected for one of the Women's Super League Academies.

At 17 years old players can be offered a professional contract.

Future Footballers

What's next?
Most professional players retire by the age of 35 and will find new jobs, such as working in football or the media.

For more information visit: www.thefa.com

Make a Table Football
▶ activity

Ask an adult to help with steps 2 and 3.

1 Draw a pitch on green paper with a white pencil and stick it in the bottom of a shoe box.

2 Cut goal holes in both ends of the box.

3 Push four long cocktail sticks through the box. Put blutack or tape on one end of each stick to create handles.

4 Paint the tops of five clothes pegs in one colour, and five in another. Clip them on to the cocktail sticks in the team arrangements shown here.

Get a small lightweight ball, like a ping pong ball and now you are ready to play!

Football for Everyone

Blind Football
▶ *listen up*

✳ How Many Players?

Five. Four outfields and one goalie.

Outfield players are blind.

Goalie is not blind, but he must never leave the goalkeeper area.

✳ How to Play

The ball has small metal balls inside it, so it makes a noise as it rolls.

The goalie can shout instructions, as well as a guide, who stands behind the goal, saying when to shoot the ball.

✳ Special Rules

Players must shout 'voy' before tackling another player.

Spectators must be quiet, so the players can hear the ball.

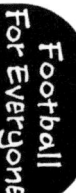

Amputee Football
▶ speedy crutches

✳ How Many Players?
Seven. Six outfields and one goalie.

All outfield players have two arms, but one leg and use metal crutches to move around.

Goalie can have two legs, but only one arm.

✳ How to Play
Can only use leg to kick the ball, not crutches.

✳ Special Rules
Goalie cannot leave the penalty area.

No slide tackles.

Cannot use crutches to hit another player.

Amputee means you have lost part of your body, either when you were born, or in an accident.

Football For Everyone

Powerchair Football
▶ wheels of fortune

✹ How Many Players?
Four. Goalkeeper, Centre, two Wingers. All players have limited movement and require a wheelchair to move around.

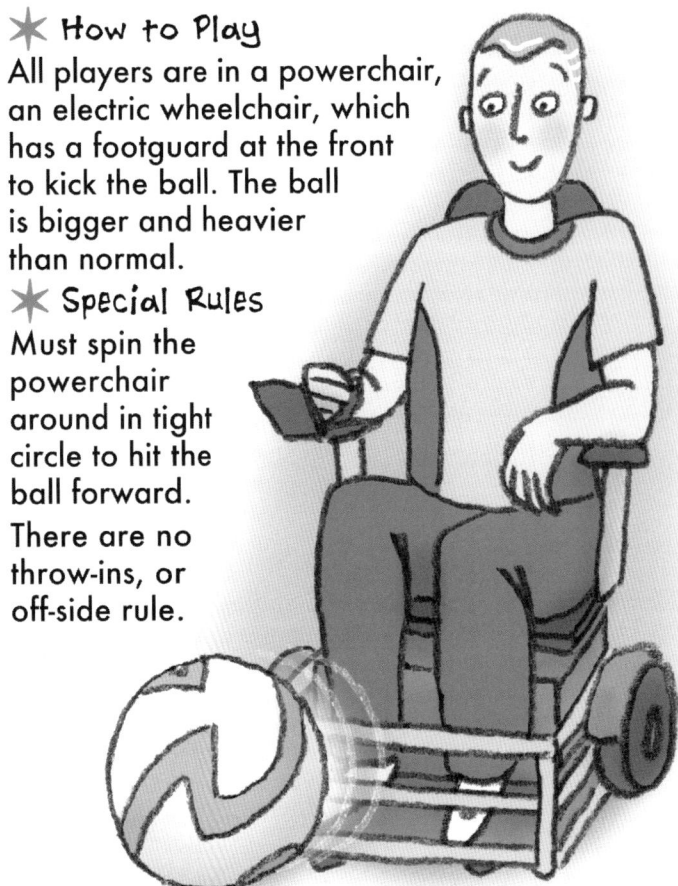

✹ How to Play
All players are in a powerchair, an electric wheelchair, which has a footguard at the front to kick the ball. The ball is bigger and heavier than normal.

✹ Special Rules
Must spin the powerchair around in tight circle to hit the ball forward.

There are no throw-ins, or off-side rule.